Caithness & Sutherland
Trout Loch Country

by
Lesley Crawford

D1470986

DEDICATION

To Ronnie for his quiet encouragement and to Andrew, Kelly and Prince for trying to keep quiet!

CAITHNESS AND SUTHERLAND

TROUT LOCH COUNTRY

BY

LESLEY CRAWFORD

Published by:
North of Scotland Newspapers, 42 Union Street, Wick,
Caithness, Scotland.

ACKNOWLEDGEMENTS

I must thank the following for their invaluable assistance:— Jill Mackay — terrific typing and translation of scribbles. David Cathcart — Superior Line Drawings, North of Scotland Newspapers, Caithness Tourist Board, Harpers Fly Fishing Services and Pentland Sports Emporium — and all the local anglers, keepers and ghillies I have met over the years. — Their patient advice has been freely given and has helped considerably in the construction of this work.

MAP COURTESY OF DREW JAMIESON, "ANGLERS COMPANIONS" EDINBURGH.

ALL PHOTOGRAPHS FROM THE CRAWFORD COLLECTION (L.C. & R.W. CRAWFORD)

FRONT COVER: Loch Calder, Caithness.

BACK COVER: The Author on Loch Loyal, Sutherland.

ISBN 1 871704 05 7

Typeset by North of Scotland Newspapers,
42 Union Street, Wick Caithness, Scotland.
Printed by Highland News Group Limited, Henderson Road, Inverness, Scotland.

CONTENTS

FOREWORD BY ROY EATON, FREELANCE EDITOR.

Roy Eaton is the Consulting Editor of 'Salmon Trout and Sea-trout' and is a former editor of 'Trout and Salmon', 'Where to Fish', 'Fishing Magazine' and was Chief Sub Editor of 'The Field' for several years.

DISCLAIMER

This book is meant to be as up to date as possible for the 1990's. We do however, live in a time of great change and lochs can 'change hands' just as the quality of fishing can alter for a variety of complex reasons. One thing is certain however, Caithness and Sutherland together can offer an almost infinite number of good quality trout lochs and as long as you seek permission and fish fairly, the visiting angler will always be assured of a warm Highland welcome.

FOREWORD
TROUT LOCH COUNTRY

No matter how many times I drive north from Inverness, once I have crossed Struie Hill and left Bonar Bridge behind, I never fail to experience a vague feeling of unease. It seems always to be accentuated by two long stretches of straight road before and after Golspie. Six hundred miles from home, I invariably wonder: What am I doing here? Where am I going? Then, with Brora passed, and Helmsdale, and as the car climbs up to the Ord of Caithness, where the mountains meet the sea, the feeling fades. By the time the 'Welcome-to-Caithness' sign is passed, and the car is descending Berriedale Braes, I feel that I, a Sassenach, a Londoner no less, am coming home.

That is the effect that Caithness has on people who like wild and lonely places interspersed with just sufficient habitation to provide their everyday needs and any craving they may have for human contact. That is the effect the county must have had on Lesley Crawford and her family to make them forsake city life and make their home on Scotland's far north coast.

They live at Reay, midway between Dunnet Head, mainland Britain's northern-most cape, and Strathy Point, which lies like a clenched fist, forefinger extended into the northern ocean. Behind them is a vast and magnificent hinterland, bleakly beautiful, inhospitable, treeless (at least, it was treeless until the foresters despoiled so many thousands of acres): the Flow Country of Caithness and the rugged outcrops and peaks of north-west Sutherland, scattered with trout lochs as though from a pepper-pot, crossed by rivers and burns, every one of them holding trout or salmon or sea-trout, or perhaps all three. It was a wilderness which the Crawfords found very attractive, she for the fishing, he for the walking; both for the solitude.

It is this wealth of fishing for 'wild' brown trout, unadulterated by stew-reared 'stockies', which Lesley Crawford describes in <u>Trout Loch Country</u> to guide newcomers and sometimes literally to keep them on the right track. If as many follow her advice as I think will do so, I shall have one regret; their presence will leave less room for me. On the other hand, if they like what they find, they will come to love and respect Caithness and Sutherland exactly as I do. That will be no bad thing, and I shall grudge them nothing.

ROY EATON
PETERBOROUGH

August 1990

Lesley Crawford with fine basket of wild Highland trout.

INTRODUCTION

Any cursory glance at an Ordnance Survey Map of the Far North reveals an absolute myriad of trouting waters, large or small, roadside or remote, fertile and green or dark and foreboding. All will have their own special attraction and visiting anglers, and for that matter those more familiar, are often overwhelmed by the choice of angling delights awaiting them!

This Guide attempts to throw as much light as possible upon the tantalising subjects — From the lochs, the terrain and the all important weather, to how to catch the fish and where best to try. It has been lovingly researched and is as up to date as possible for the 1990's.

I would make no bones about the fact that I love my fishing with a great intensity, and, just as others care passionately about their golf or squash game, I do so about my angling. I find it fundamental to my enjoyment of life. It is my 'hydro-therapy', relaxing, invigorating and challenging. Tiresome and frustrating at times too, but never boring!

So I do hope that within these pages the true pleasure of fly fishing for trout in the Highlands will shine through and to this end I have included as much the enjoyment of the mountains and straths, the wildlife and the wilderness, as well as the essential technicalities of the water themselves. In my opinion they intrinsically add as much joy to a days outing as the capture of a truly wild trout.

The guide has been packed with little nuggets of information only the 'locals' know, as well as lots of friendly advice and I hope it brings you much enjoyment and as many fish to your rod as you would wish for!

—— O ——

THE COUNTIES AND THEIR CHARACTER

Caithness and Sutherland are two greatly contrasting counties making up the most northerly reaches of Scotland.

Caithness with its rolling moors, heather and peat, and the well publicised 'Flow Country' studded with the dubh (black) lochs holds a special charm for those liking the wide open spaces. Admittedly it is at times a little bleak, for the landscape is one of a vast wilderness stretching infinitely into the distance. It is not without some hills however, and the 'Scarabens' loom up from sea level in the southern wastes of the Caithness hinterland. It is definitely a place to enjoy expansive horizons in comtemplative solitude. It can offer a complete escape from traffic jams, motorways, noise and pollution and that is an essential part of its character and fascination.

Sutherland on the other hand is a much larger and more mountainous region, stretching from Cape Wrath in the far North West corner down the West coast as far as Lochinver and across the central area to the Kyle of Sutherland on the East coast. The mountains of Ben Loyal, Hope and Foinaven tower in the North and the sugar loafed Suilven, Canisp and Quinag dominate the West. Ben Klibreck and Ben More Assynt lie above the lochs in the central region. Between the hills are great fertile straths notably Strath Naver, Kildonan and Halladale. Dotted along these lie the remnants of the crofts abandoned during the Clearances and they are a tragic reminder to an all too colourful past. When you visit these areas reflect a while on the tumbled heaps of stones for they were once great crofting communities before the Clearances for sheep farming and the grim potato famine drove them out. The Clearance village of Rossal in Strathnaver has been preserved as a dark memory of the Highlanders sad history and is recommended for those wishing to know more about the subject.

The lochs of the two counties have very differing characteristics and there is quite literally something to suit all angling tastes. From the icy blue richness of a limestone loch at Durness to a dark peaty tarn high in the hills, and from a secluded moorland loch to a loch in the midst of farming country. Nearly all will contain wild brown trout and these vary in size from a few ounces to several pounds in weight. Salmon and sea-trout may also be caught in a loch providing there is a reasonable link with the sea. Remember there are very few if any 'coarse' fish present neither are there many 'rainbows', so native game fish will nearly always be the quarry unless otherwise stated. All the fish however give great account of themselves, fighting hard and giving a good rod doubling battle before surrender. Fly only is predominently the rule but with a little skill and patience the fish rise readily to the fly and it is well worth perservering.

Both counties are ones to fall in love with and many visitors return year

Glen Lochs: Caithness and Sutherland border.

after year. There is a good network of roads giving access to all but the very remote parts making touring around the area pleasant and easy. The landscape round every corner constantly changes and delights and at times can be breathtakingly beautiful. All this and superlative fishing what more could an angler wish for?

—— O ——

THE WEATHER

In all angling fraternities there is never a subject more discussed or berated than the weather! "Its too bright, hot, cold, sunny, misty, wet!" are cries familiar to all of us. In the most general of terms 'good' trout fishing conditions are cloudy, mild with a stiff breeze rippling the water. However, it is possible to catch fish in all sorts of weather including northerly gales, rain, sleet or hot sunshine! It is such a fickle topic I shall deal first with the conditions I prefer not to go out in...

a) Glaring 'brassy' sunshine with clear blue skies and no cloud — I rarely catch any fish in these conditions except for suicidal fingerlings.

b) Thick mist or fog which is unlikely to clear. — The diffuse 'white light' from the mist seems always to put the fish 'down'.

c) Exceptionally high winds causing a conditions known locally as 'cats paws' on the water. The surface of the loch takes on a spattered appearance and casting becomes back breaking. I usually go home!

d) Flat calms — without any ripple my intentions become far too obvious but it may still be just possible to capture a fish or two if it is dull and the fish are moving well.

The Changing Seasons

When trying to assess what to expect at certain times of the year it is prudent to remember that in the Far North we are 'right next to' the elements and that one can literally encounter a mass of differing weather all in the one day! For example:— Opening day March 15, 1989 had heavy rain, gales, blizzards (two!), sleet and some blue sky and bright sunshine!

However here are some general guidelines to follow...

March 15 to end April —

Early season trouting in the North is very much 'pot luck', some years these months are mild and very productive and others appallingly cold with snow and sleet and biting winds with hardly a fish caught. The bigger overwintered fish are close to the banks but is essential to have a warm day to tempt them.

May and June —

The weather in these months usually begins to settle and it becomes much warmer and drier. Droughts often occur and water levels can fall dramatically. Long spells of sunshine often prevail and although this is lovely for touring and seeing the countryside at its best, weather which is both hot and bright will tend to put the fish down. Occasionally temperatures up to the 80°'s are recorded as in June 1989 and early May 1990.

July and August —

These are traditionally mild and wet months with rainfall picking up and better fishing conditions usually returning. Good catches are recorded on the 'grey' days but I personally have always found the last two weeks or so in August to be inexplicably dour, before the fishing picks up again in the 'back end'.

September and October —

September is my favourite fishing month with the bigger fish moving in to the shore to make for the spawning redds. It can get very cold with sleet showers but a pleasantly warm autumnal day with its lovely coppery hues, makes for excellent fishing prospects. Most lochs close their doors on October 6 but those with a sea-trout run such as the loch of Wester in East Caithness stay open until October 31. I always fish right up until closing day and have taken some very large fish in October given a mild spell.

I am a firm believer in the theory that the weather is the crucial variable which will determine the success of a days outing. One can narrow the odds by selecting a good trouting loch and perfecting all the skills and tactics required for loch style fishing but the overiding factor of what is going on 'above your head' remains. And of course it is the one thing we have no control over though conveniently it is always there to take the blame if things are not going well! For the visitor with his holiday booked months ahead I can offer this advice... On the days of cloud, warmth and a good wind fish your chosen lochs 'to the hilt' as surprisingly these ideal conditions occur only infrequently. On the not so good days be prepared to experiment with trips at differing times of the day, or late into the night if necessary. Remember in the North there is little or no darkness at night in the summer months so the full 24 hours are at your angling disposal! I particularly enjoy fishing in the very early morning. The roads and lochs are empty of people and it is as if you are entirely at one with your environment and its magnificent solitude.

Finally, while the weather plays a major role in determining fishing quality it is not the 'be all and end all' and there is always a day to confound the experts! So if you are 'there' it is always worth having a go, you may just be able to rewrite the text books and if not you can always blame 'IT' — I know I frequently do!

—— O ——

THE WILDLIFE

As you fish you will come across a host of bird life to delight the eye. Many of the larger lochs have over wintering geese present and booming out their calls from the far reaches they are a constant reminder whether it is early or late in the season. Curlews, lapwings, skylark, grouse, herons, pheasant and all type of duck are here in profusion along with the more rare red and black throated diver, greenshank, dunlin and golden plover. Birds of prey are often seen soaring overhead. Muting buzzards, and in Sutherland, the magnificent golden eagle will occasionally be glimpsed. Hen Harriers criss-cross fields in seach of food and kestrels and merlins are also quite common. — Binoculars are a must if you enjoy bird watching while on a fishing outing!

Herds of deer roam the remoter hillsides and I have often 'rounded the corner' of a lonely hill loch to come face to face with hinds and their young at the waters edge. Otters too put in a rare appearance. I once had that peculiar feeling that I was 'not alone' while fishing on my local loch. Up from the depths came the head and shoulders of a large dog otter which at first I thought a seal until rationality prevailed! — It was Loch Calder after all, miles from the sea, and not an adjoining river or burn in sight! He bobbed his head a few times and watched somewhat scornfully my feeble attempts to attract some fish before flipping over and disappearing with a haughty splash.

In Sutherland I had my one and only glimpse of a wild cat near Lochinver but to the rear of my house in Caithness my husband came upon the mysterious puma-like black cat known to roam the remoter areas of the Northern Highlands. It is hard to say who had the bigger shock but the cat bounded away into the heather at a tremendous rate! Its size would compare with that of a small labrador dog. I hasten to add that my husband was fell running at the time and had not consumed anything stronger than tea prior to his strange encounter!

Whatever you see at the loch, in the hills or on the moors accept it all as part of the rich tapestry which is Highland fishing. Please leave them untouched and undisturbed for all to savour, and then they can only add to yours and future generations enjoyment of a days outing in our regions.

—— O ——

Cock Pheasant.

PLANTLIFE

What you will find in the way of 'flora and fauna' depends very much on the area in which your chosen loch is situated, and also on your own powers of observation as few of the wild plants on view are obviously large. The ferocious winters with, at times, hurricane force winds, mean the indigenous plants must be ground hugging and hardy in order to survive, but discovering them in their remote habitats can still give great pleasure nevertheless.

Around the fertile lochs set in rich farmland water iris and marsh marigolds blaze in profusion at the waters edge. Reddish water avens can also be seen and celandines will often be found under any trees, while the yellow gorse and broom is common particularly along feeder streams. The wild rhodedendron, now considered a pest in some quarters, adds great splashes of colour to the landscape. On the calmer more mud based lochs oval lily pads with their cupped flowers spread out and harebell and wild stock also inhabit the hedgerows.

Going out on to the moors the more delicate flowers and shrubs are replaced in the main by heather, bracken and fern — while writing I offer a cautionary note on bracken — recent research has indicated at certain times of the year that the spores of this plant are cancer inducing. Should you have to walk through such bracken put a scarf or similar over your nose and mouth so as not to inhale the spores which become airborne as you walk. Late August and September seem to be the worst times so be warned. — Ling and bell heather mix with rowan, birch and whin in the more sheltered glens, often leading right down to the loch shore. Nestling amongst all this will be a number of alpine plants to delight the eye. Wild orchids, saxifrages, vetch and bog violets are common and amongst the shrub like species are the lovely creeping willow, banks of wild thyme, and here and there bilberries or blaeberries as they are more commonly known.

Bilberry

16

The little purple berries of this particular plant are delicious when in season (usually September) as are brambles if you can stand the prickles!

In the more boggy peat and wetland environs, also known to many now as the 'Flow Country', the lovely spagnum moss with its soft pastel shades, springs beneath your feet along with wild sedge, purple bog thistles and the ubiquitous bog cotton which is always an indication to tread warily. Throughout the moor wild grasses, some extremely rare, all add to this rich tapestry of plantlife.

Up in the more mountainous regions, walk carefully as you may just be lucky enough to come across 'Primula Scotica' or Scots primrose, a tiny purple leaved alpine flower. Moss campion and the pretty little Globe flower, which resembles a large buttercup, can be found clinging to rocky hillsides and amongst the rough grass the tiny blue flowers of the milkwort may now and then be seen.

I think that one of the most charming and most often ignored 'plants' (it is not strictly a plant) is the lichen. The intricate variety of textures and colours to be seen as it weaves a slow intricate web over stone and wood creates a strange raw beauty all of its own. With many of these odd 'plants' over a thousand years old, I often pause at a lochside to reflect on just what this hardiest of species must have seen and gone through.

Just as with the wildlife please leave our plants photographed but undisturbed, many have a considerable lifetime ahead of them after all! Throughout the seasons from when the first spring flowers appear to the autumnal riot of purple heather adhorning our hillsides they can only add to the enjoyment of a days fishing, and provide as much interest to the serious botanist as to the angler.

—— ◯ ——

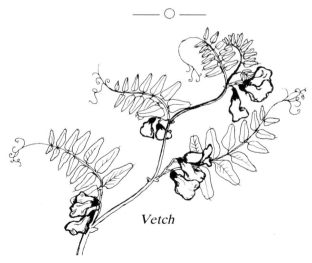

Vetch

SOME TECHNICALITIES OF THE LOCH TERRAIN

It goes without saying that what is in, on, around and at the bottom of the loch will directly affect its fishing.

On arriving at an 'unknown' loch it is often a great help to run through this simple checklist:—

a) *The water — what 'colour' is it and what depth?*
b) *The Bank — what are the surrounds like?*
c) *The Bottom — is is possible to wade?*

Local experts are often able to assess the quality of fishing potential from these factors alone, but to assist the less familiar here are a few more guidelines...

The Water

The water in the lochs of Caithness and Sutherland will greatly vary in colour, tint, depth and ability to sustain fish growth and degree (if any) of sedimentation.

If not completely gin clear the waters will vary from a pale tea-stain to a rich sherry stain or even darker in some cases. The cause of this staining is the degree of peat content to be found in the water. Occasionally as in the limestone lochs of Durness there is no peat discolouration and the water is startlingly clear. You should always bear in mind however that water which is so crystal clear, while being a delight to wade, can often be very difficult to fish. If you can 'see the fish' then the fish most certainly can see you and a good wind helps mightily to disguise your intentions! As the cause of the 'tea-stain' is usually the leaching of peat materials, why then, on the boggy moors of the 'Flow Country', are there lochs of excellent clarity? The reason for this more often than not is that they are spring-fed on a sandstone base and these are waters of very good quality holding many a large fish. These springs are often known as Chalybeate springs and are natural waters containing iron salts in solution, look out for their presence on Ordnance Survey Maps.

The water will of course sustain all the weed, algae and other organisms necessary to provide good feeding for the trout. — It is often quite possible to fish two lochs side by side, one holding small fish of three to the pound, and the other holding great 'whoppers'. Therefore, where the fish have good growth rates there will also be good feeding and an abundance of plant and weed growth with all the attendant insect, shrimp, minnow and mollusc life. So examine your loch carefully for any weed beds as here the bigger, better fed fish will lie. Interestingly in Fraser Darlings book 'Natural History In The Highlands & Islands' the theory is purported that it is the lochs with the poorest spawning areas ie 'redds' which have the biggest fish in them, and those with excellent

18

spawning have a preponderance of small fish — I leave you to make your own decision on this!

The only kind of loch water I would absolutely avoid would be one which has become sedimented — the simple reason being that I have yet to catch a fish in one! If the water is opaque, cloudy or muddy with visible particles suspended in it then it is better to change lochs (easily done) than thrash away at something so unforgiving! The causes of this discolouration are usually the very high winds occuring in the North which stir up the bottom particularly of the shallower lochs, leaving everything literally 'in the soup' before the mud settles again. I freely admit to never having taken a fish from such a water but if you have I would be delighted to know which fly you used?

The depth of the water will usually determine where the trout are likely to be and thus most fish are caught where 'warm' meets 'cold'. Anglers will therefore be seen while wading to be casting from shallows into deeper water, or if in a boat, fishing from the deeps into the shallower bays. — I particularly like wading lochs which are gently shelving and can usually be found hovering on their shores more than any other! By wading along the bank in a 'zig-zag' fashion thus . . . .

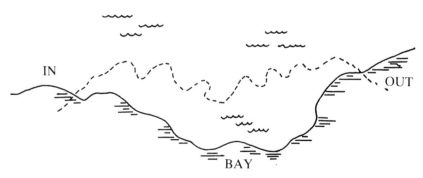

I would hope to cover most fish lying in a depth of between 3 to 10ft. Some lochs have deep water very close to the edge so wading is unnecessary and with a little stealth one may be rewarded with a very large fish close to the bank.

Useful 'rules of thumb' for *Assessing the Water*:—

— Light water, light coloured fly
— Dark water, dark fly
— "The clearer the water the Bigger the Fish"

Banks and Bottoms

What is around a loch will more often than not determine its quality. For example the rich fertile farmland of East Caithness holds many productive lochs such as Watten, Stemster and St Johns. Moorland lochs too can hold good fish particularly those with heather banks which hold a mass of winged insects. Given a favourable wind big fish will move in to snap these up, likewise in 'cattle country' where the cow dung fly makes a tasty addition to the trouts diet. The more remote hill lochs are nearly all surrounded by a mixture of heather, rough grass and boulders and the quality of trout will be dependent on the feeding available as previously discussed.

The loch bottoms will also give good indication as to what is within. White limestone, pale marl or shingle and sandstone are the most favoured in the North and all will have large trout present. The only lochs I would really avoid are those with dangerously boggy, peat-hagged banks and very dark almost treacle stained water. I have never found fish of any size present in them but there are usually some there for those willing to try!

——— ○ ———

Sundew

FINDING THE FISH

One of the greatest difficulties for our visitors seems to be in the actual location of the trout, an ailment which can afflict us all from time to time, hardened locals included! Thankfully there are a few simple guidelines to help the quest along...

Keep uppermost in your mind when approaching the lochs that if you can find a loch with rich trout food sources you will find the fish and often some very large ones at that! Compare for example the rich, fertile clear waters of shallow Loch Watten with a deep peaty dubh loch and observe their very differing trout sizes and quality — The sleek silvery Loch Leven strain of the well fed Watten trout bears little resemblance to the skinny black fingerlings of a dark dubh loch. But there are a myriad of trout waters 'in between' these two extremes, each with its own subtle variations. Indeed the almost infinite diversity of lochs can be delightfully bewildering! — Gentle moorland lochs or isolated mountain 'tarns', green fields or wild heathery banks, the choice is yours. The 'better' lochs of Caithness and Sutherland will always have some, if not all, of the salient features shown on the sketch below, so there follows a simple guide around a typical Highland shoreline...

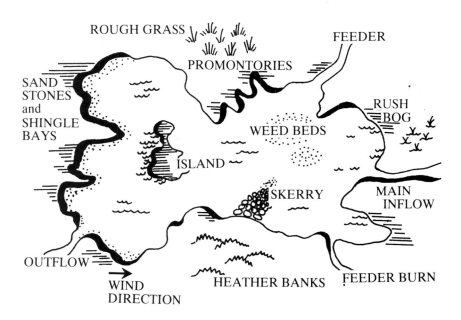

ROUGH GRASS

PROMONTORIES

FEEDER

SAND
STONES
and
SHINGLE
BAYS

RUSH
BOG

WEED BEDS

ISLAND

SKERRY

MAIN
INFLOW

OUTFLOW

WIND
DIRECTION

HEATHER BANKS

FEEDER BURN

It is a good idea to start off in the shallower shingle bays with the wind behind. Visitors are usually tempted to rush to the nearest promontory, but if its mid season and the grass is heavily trodden many have had the same idea before you! — Fish the bays carefully but do not linger overlong as this type of wind direction gives poor fly presentation especially of a fly which is 'all wing and no hackle'. The trout feed facing into wind and if you are casting straight at them they end up looking at the 'hook end' rather than seeing its shape side on. If the wind is 'behind' I would recommend a bushy, palmered/hackled fly such as the Bibio, Goats Toe, Loch Ordie or a large Zulu.

Next tackle the promontories casting as far out to the island as possible. The 'side' wind will now aid fly presentation considerably. If the edges of these plunge straight into cold deep water fish the sides carefully as the fish usually lie where deep meets shallow. These promontories and islands give attractive food holding areas with their underwater 'currents' bringing in mollusc, shrimp, nymph and fly to the waiting trout, and as I said 'where there's food, there's fish'.

On to the weed beds as some of the biggest trout can usually be found there. Cast carefully around the <u>edges</u> of the weed or as near to them as you can. You will often be rewarded with a fat trout lying next to his convenient shelter and foodstore.

Any inflows or feeder burns should be given attention really only early and late in the season when fish are showing interest in the spawning. A 'maiden' fish (a non spawning hen) in March is delicious and truly a prize to grace your table but end of season gravid hens or kyped males are not really my choice though they are often fished for because of their extra weight. In mid season the burns seem to attract only small immature fish and are not really worth bothering about for any length of time.

Now we can walk past the wind blown bog and rushes to the heathery banks — how I wish the gales always blew so conveniently! — Stomp up

Wild Brown Trout.

22

through the heather as it contains abundant fly life especially in warm weather and you would be surprised as to what comes up to have a look at it. The Bibio, Grouse and Claret, Wickhams, Invicta all bring success off heather clad shores.

Do not omit the skerries, even if they are a bit difficult to wade. Some will be submergd, some bare and exposed but all will be worth a cast as some very good fish can be taken off these rocks. The collection of stone and boulders hold good food stores such as snails, nymphs and minnows so wade carefully and it may produce the best fish of the day.

Choose an overcast day with a good breeze to visit this typical loch. Examine your first fish carefully. Is it long headed black and thin, indicitive of poor feeding, or is it gold or silver bellied with small head and plump deep body? It it is one of the former it is often better to change lochs if larger fish are your chosen quarry. Remember with so many to choose from that it can be easily done! For those who want a serious challenge head for those clear watered, fertile and shallow indented lochs of the Far North for they can produce memorable fish in splendid surroundings.

—— O ——

THE EFFECTS OF COMMERCIAL AFFORESTATION

This prickly issue must unfortunately raise its head in any description of the lochs and their surroundings for there is so much of it now in Caithness and Sutherland. Interested parties in the 'PRO' corner include Fountain Forestry, various Lords, lairds and other estate owners and in the 'ANTI' corner the Nature Conservancy Council, RSPB, Friends of the Earth, Scottish Wildland Group, local author Bruce Sandison et al!

Most people who have never been to the Far North would argue that planting trees 'is a good thing' and if I did not live here I would be inclined to agree with them. It is only when you drive up somewhere like Strath Halladale for example, does the full extent of industrial afforestation hit you very hard indeed. Massive long ditches with stumpy conifers atop score the wilderness for mile after mile. Forget any romantic notions of a 'stroll in the forest', other than on the forestry road network it is virtually impossible to cross the moorland. And once the sitka spruce grow, if indeed they grow at all, another well documented bone of contention, you will not be able to penetrate the dense canopy, the trees being so close together. As far as the angling is concerned the tree planters now own the rights to a considerable number of trout lochs. How the actual planting process has affected the quality of the fishing in the lochs remains a heatedly controversial issue, my own opinion being that any massive upheaval in the environment surrounding a loch and its feeder streams and spawning redds, cannot do it a great deal of good, if not considerable harm.

Local people have on the whole remained tolerant in allowing Fountain Forestry into their midst. Many have balked however, myself included, at the vast amounts of money being made via tax concessions and other government grants to TV celebrities, snooker players and those of that ilk. Indeed few investors if any, show the slightest concern for what is happening to a once vast and lonely wilderness, 'Flow Country' or not. Is it such a sad reflection of todays monetarist age that the capitalization of an investment always takes precedent over the preservation of 'a bit of bog and a few birds'? Forestry is a powerful force invested in by very powerful people and little of their profit in real terms seems to be ploughed back here. The NCC are trying their best to halt the relentless march of the conifer by declaring areas SSSI's but then the ridiculous situation arises of landowners demanding vast sums of money as compensation for NOT planting trees!

I leave you the reader to make up your own mind though I would recommend the NCC leaflet 'Peatlands of Caithness and Sutherland' or 'Nature Conservation and Afforestation in Britain' (NCC). Also John McEwans' 'Who Owns Scotland', which contains a frank and telling section on forestry investment.

—— O ——

THE EQUIPMENT

Very often I see visitors come here armed to the teeth with poker stiff reservoir rods or even spinning rods; lures of hideous variety and a lot of other very expensive equipment totally unnecessary for loch style fishing. — The key to success in fly fishing our lochs is to stay as simple and as lightweight as possible. That basically means a light flexible carbon based rod, 10ft is usually the favoured length, lightweight reel, double tapered matching DFM floating line and nylon of 4-6lb breaking strain. In the fly box all that is really required is a reasonable selection of wet fly favourites. These include...

Invicta	Black Pennel
Soldier Palmer	Bibio
Wickhams Fancy	Ke-He
Zulu	Kingfisher Butcher
Butchers (Various)	Teal Blue and Silver
Black and Peacock Spider	Conemara Black
Blue Zulu	Silver Invicta
Dunkeld	Grouse and Claret

Traditional Wet Fly
(Palmered)

Traditional Wet Fly
(Winged)

More specialist flies would include the 'Dry Daddy' and big bushy flies such as the Loch Ordie and the Goats Toe from Orkney. Nymphs in assorted colours also have a corner in my box particularly for early season work.

Fly sizes favoured here are 10, 12, and 14 with most locals using 12's. Everyone will have their own personal selection amongst the above list, but if I were to choose three flies that bring the best results, I would plump for the Wickhams Fancy, the Zulu and the Pennel, but if you have your own favourites, use what you put the most faith in!

Other bits and pieces include a light canvas tackle bag, lightweight folding waders so that you can walk a good way without excessive fatigue, plenty of food and a hot drink. A map and compass are essential if you venture off the beaten track, mists can suddenly descend and getting lost and floundering around in bog should not be taken lightly.

I always wear sunglasses — even on a dull day I find staring into the dancing water very tiring and a great strain on the eyes. As I wear glasses anyway I use poloroid clip-ons, but for the less myopic sunglasses are a recommended protection from eye strain and that dangerous stray fly as you are casting.

Scissors are a profound nuisance; I recently changed to using nail clippers on a lanyard around my neck and find them much easier to use and I don't keep loosing them in the heather!

Landing nets come into the 'heavy' category. Unless you are going all day in the boat where they are essential I recommend leaving them at home! They are cumbersome and awkward and I find most fish can be easily beached providing they are fully played out and turned on their side. However if you think using one gives you more confidence by all means take one with you.

Clothing should be warm, dark coloured but not so restrictively heavy that you are exhausted after three casts! I use the layer system. In a boat as many layers as are humanly possible, there is no shelter once afloat. On the bank I adjust the layers much more putting on or taking off a jersey accordingly. A good waterproof (waxed cotton or the lighter but more expensive Goretex) is always required as is a hat to keep your ears covered in the gales! In ferocious gales a balaclava is recommended as it does not blow off. On cold days fingerless mitts are another of my preferences, flies somehow always get caught up in ordinary gloves. Early and late season most anglers are not without some thermal underwear, there is nothing worse than being chilled to the bone but if you are 'macho' enough to do without them, go ahead!

A 'priest' is the last thing always to be carried, preferably in a pocket rather than at the bottom of the tackle bag! They dispatch the fish quickly rather than hunting around for suitable stones.

I would emphasise that the capital outlay on your equipment should match the amount of use you intend to give it, unless you are very wealthy! Very often I am confronted at the loch with persons on holiday 'dressed to kill' and with extraordinarily expensive rods and yet their catches are no better or worse than mine. Which brings me to...

—— O ——

TACTICS

"It ain't what you fish — its the way that you fish it!"

One may come to the Far North equipped with the best tackle and clothing that money can buy and yet be unable to catch many of the indigenous wild brown trout. This is because the style of angling on a Highland loch is greatly different from the 'rainbow' reservoir techniques, to which many of our visitors are more accustomed.

'Loch Style' Fishing Tactics.

At any loch bank it is always possible to tell the local expert from the casual visitor.

The former will be casting away methodically, and, with minimal effort be putting out a shortish line working his way along the bank, retrieving the fly quickly to GIVE IT LIFE, and keeping the rod point on the retrieve very low. His line will be kept as straight as possible keeping him in touch with his flies and if he feels a fish or sees a swirl where his flies are, he will lift and tighten quickly but not savagely. He is constantly attentive, looking and listening, watching the water for an unusual movement and straining his ears for the distinctive 'bloop' of a heavy fish moving.

The casual fisher or those less experienced, will often stick out like the proverbial sore thumb! He will be transfixed to the one spot with his rod pointing skyward and he will be busy watching the end of his line for some peculiar reason! — Remember the line does not catch the fish the fly does, so look out 'over' the water to where the fly is and await the action there. — This chaps flies hang lifelessly in the water and when he does lift off to cast there is much swishing of the rod and flashing of line back and forth. "You'll no catch onything wi' your flee birling aboot yer lugs" was the cutting advice given to me by a ghillie on the subject of 'false casting'! (Translation — you will not catch anything with your fly in mid air all the time, instead of on the water.) Likewise it is essential to keep moving along the bank — GO TO THE FISH, THE FISH WILL NOT COME TO YOU —.

The native browns will have specific 'lies' rather like a salmon, and by moving down the bank one is covering fresh lies all the time. The rainbow trout of the South are a shoaling fish and move around the loch quite conveniently which means standing in the one spot for long enough will eventually bring some reward! Not so the Caithness and Sutherland brownies, keep moving and given the right conditions you will almost certainly catch fish.

The fish are extremely fast and can be 'on' and 'off' the fly before you know it so that is why we keep the rod point very low (parallel to the water) while hand lining in the flies. This absorbs the shock of the take

27

and gives a good striking 'arm'. Strike if you can, at the swirl, by 'feeling' for the fish and then upping the rod to 90° quickly but not brutally. You want to sink the barb not break the trouts jaw!

On the subject of casting techniques there are many excellent books already on the market going into great detail on the various casting skills.

I do not propose to give a long dissertation on how to cast a fly. Instead I would emphasise keeping your technique as fluid and as simple as possible! See casting sequence in the photographs, 11a to 11e.

The best at 'casting' do not make the best 'fishers' and vice versa, my advice would be to think of casting as a way of getting your flies on the water rather than some refined art form or, alternatively, an exhaustive, arm breaking process! A lot of heaving, sweating and crashing of lines is tiring and fish scaring and remember the ghillies advice on keeping the flies on the water rather than in the air. One point to note however is that many of the lochs have high banks behind and learning to roll cast or steeple cast, as well as the traditional overhead cast, will save a lot of time and temper! — Above all go to the lochs to enjoy yourself. It does not matter if your casting leaves a bit to be desired. — Three people at a loch here would be considered a crowd so you are unlikely to have an audience for that hashed cast or that fly caught in the heather anyway!

Three people at a Loch is considered a crowd.

Boat or Bank?

Many local anglers in the Counties prefer to fish by boat if there is one available, rather than off the bank. The reasons for using a boat would be:

a) to cover a lot more water especially if the loch is large or has dangerous banks in parts.
b) The very enjoyable 'escape' on to the water leaving terra firma behind for a while.

Disadvantages in using a boat include:

a) the well known law 'if anything can go wrong in a boat it will'! — That encompasses such mishaps as tangled tackle, your own, and with your partners, loosing oars, rollocks, fly-boxes over the side, the outboard failing to start, going aground on skerries at the vital moment and so on ad infinitum!
b) It can get bitterly cold sitting in a boat for hours on end, no matter how many layers of clothing you put on.
c) Boats can be dangerous. Falling into deep icy cold water can be fatal and to this end I would advise against going out on a deep loch alone, or, standing up in the boat to cast.

All in all I much prefer wading. It is much less complicated, generally safer and less costly. I love being right in touch with the water, 'at one with my element' you might say, and this to me is its main attraction coupled with the fact that I can quickly cover a rising fish again in the same area. Drifting in a boat, that opportunity has often gone 'past' before you get another chance on a different drift.

Disadvantages of wading include covering less water, flies being caught behind at the crucial time, and wading on slippery rocks or boggy ground is not really advised, though you are more likely to get a 'ducking' rather than a 'drowning'.

Both methods are enjoyable however, and providing you take reasonable care and no unnecessary risks, both can be participated in safely.

Nylon and Flies — What to Use.

The traditional loch fly CAST (the nylon of 4-6 lbs BS) is usually around 12-15ft in length, to which are attached 3 flies on droppers, at intervals approx 3ft apart. This is the only area in which I depart from tradition. I use only one or two flies on a leader of 10ft. My reasons for this are simple. I do not believe the trout an intellectual creature able to distinguish between a Black Pennel and a Black and Peacock Spider however I do believe it to be a creature of instinct. Three flies crashing down in a heap of nylon simultaneously are surely more likely to appear unatural and alarming than just a single fly plopping gently into the water?

Early and late in the season I use only one fly on the point, mid season I add a dropper fly, approx 6ft from the point fly so that in the water they do not look 'related' in any way. The idea of this being that the bobfly dances attractively on the surface while the point fly sinks and searches the depths. Usually, at the beginning and end of the season, the big fish take on the point fly while in mid season they take on either as they are much more 'up' in the water and feeding at various depths, rather than bottom hugging after a cold winter.

I must also confess to having little patience with the tangled nylon and knots which often occur in a cast of three flies especially in a Caithness gale, so to prevent 'choice words' I always use only the one or two flies! And remember nylon is inexpensive but your time is <u>not</u> so change the whole thing rather than try to unpick knots.

Everyone has very differing theories on the actual choice of fly to put on. There are the various well known rules of thumb,

'Dark day = dark fly, bright day = bright fly'
OR
'Bright water = bright fly, dark water = dark fly'

and so on, but these are greatly affected by the time of year.

Simple guidelines to the wet fly seasons would be:—

March, April — Flies with 'flash' eg Kingfisher Butcher, Silver Invicta, Dunkeld.

May, June — Black fly eg Black Pennel, Black and Peacock Spider, Zulu.

July, August — Black flies with additions of brownish flies such as Wickhams Fancy, Invicta, Woodcock and Yellow.

Sept, October — Brownish flies and again the flies with 'flash' mentioned above.

At the waters edge I adhere to the choice of fly by 'colour' theory, working through the ranges black, red, silver, brown, orange until I find a colour the fish like. I do not go in much for the 'matching the hatch' theory, tending to rely more on my <u>ears</u> than entemology. If I can hear fish moving (splashs, swirls, 'bloops') then I know they are taking and that it will only be a matter of time before one hits my fly. If on the other hand there is silence and nothing moves after an hour I generally pack up and go home unless there is no option but to stay put!

There are more 'specialist' flies which can be put to good use at certain times of the year.

The use of nymphs in sizes 12-14 is a particularly good early tactic when no fish are showing on the surface. I use the traditional floating line and 10ft of nylon but with a nymph on the point. For this method I simply cast out as far as I can, let it sink and retrieve it very slowly. I have caught heavy fish to 2-3lb in weight in early April by this method. It takes patience though, and it can be a cold, mind numbing pursuit if nothing is happening. Persevere for a while however as big trout take deep on this method.

The use of the dry fly can be very killing especially in high summer. The Dry Daddy (daddy long legs) or a big bushy Loch Ordie are excellent when Crane flies or moths are present at the loch. I usually cast the 'Daddy' out as far as possible and leave it bobbing about in the ripple. I give it a gentle tweak now and again and with any luck suddenly the surface will explode and a fat trout engulf the fly in its jaws. Let the fish turn down before tightening and he is yours. Spine tingling stuff!

Finally I would say that flies very much fall in and out of vogue. One year the Zulu is the 'in' fly the next it may be the Wickhams. Do not be afraid to experiment constantly, for that is one of the great joys of fly fishing.

—— O ——

LAST HOPES

'Make not a profession of any recreation, lest your immoderate love towards it should bring a cross wish on the same.'

Col R. Venables 1662

I have always believed that the sport of trout fishing requires just as much confidence as it does skill. Confidence grows with faith in yourself, your abilities and your knowledge of the area. It also grows considerably after a red letter day, for example the capture of a 2lb trout from a difficult water, and shrinks alarmingly after a series of 'blanks'!

Various methods of keeping that all important self esteem high include; changing from a 'dour' loch to an easier 'free-rising' one for a day to stop the blanks; stopping fishing entirely for a day out with the family, re-aligns your perspective and is good 'PR' work!; re-assessing your tactics and trying to become more flexible if need be, for example switching to nymph or dry fly. — Did you take into account the weather, water colour, time of year and all the other factors previously mentioned? Without delving into the fields of superstition if you have an absolute favourite fly or prefer a 9ft rod instead of a 10ft one then by all means use it — it obviously boosts your confidence and that is essential.

If you feel your confidence is high but your loch style skills may be lacking, go and watch a local expert at work even if it is only through binoculars! What is he doing which you are not? Is the retrieve faster or slower, is he using wet or dry fly, are you using a sinking line while his is a 'floater', is his casting technique different from your own? — Has the local packed up and gone home — if so think why!

The really good angler, though I must emphasise no-one is 'perfect', richly blends his confidence and skills, constantly adapting and refining them to the changing seasons, the differing weather and the different waters. Above all do not let the capture and killing of a great number of fish take precedence over all the other joys of fishing. I try to take home (if I can) no more than half a dozen good sized fish, I never go into double figures, it gets a bit obscene somehow. I am by no means there, as some unfortunates seem to be these days just for the wholesale slaughter of a great many trout usually by illegal methods such as spinning or worming. I am there to enjoy the silence, the tranquility, the birds the mountains and the moors just as much as the fishing. If I do not succeed today well the fish are not going anywhere and theres' always another day.

Caithness and Sutherland together offer one of the last great bastions of wilderness fishing. Hopefully they will offer you a haven of peace from an otherwise troubled world. Fish the lochs fairly and philosophically, and return home relaxed and refreshed, a better angler and perhaps even a better person!

—— O ——

1. *An unusual view of the Caithness coastline from the border near Reay
   — expansive horizons are part of the joy of Caithness.*

2. The old mill at Westerdale is a familiar landmark to all anglers who fish on the Loch Dubh Estate, Caithness.

3. The Scarabens loom up in the Caithness hinterland, Loch More area of the Loch Dubh estate.

4. Sutherland is a much more mountainous region and despite the spring
   sunshine a smattering of snow flanks Ben Hee.

5. 'As you fish you will come across a host of bird life to delight the eye'
   — here black headed gulls watch the proceedings near Scrabster Loch,
   Caithness.

6. Nestling amongst wild grasses and heather lie many rare plants including spotted orchids.

7. — Wild brown trout of exceptional quality. — A 1lb 4oz Loch Watten trout caught by the author from the bank of Loch Watten on a Red Invicta, June 1990.

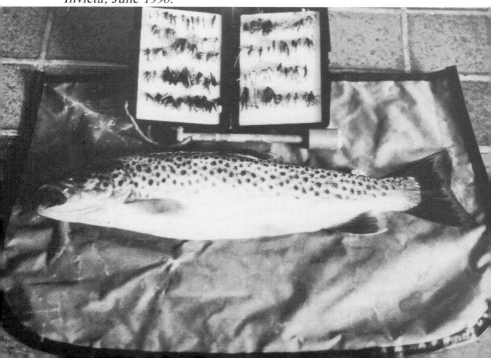

8. Keep the equipment as simple and as lightweight as possible. Angling is for all ages to enjoy — fly fishing lesson in progress, North Sutherland.

9. Local expert fly tyer Mrs Brooks of Harpers Fly Fishing Services Thurso, tying flies for use in Caithness and Sutherland.

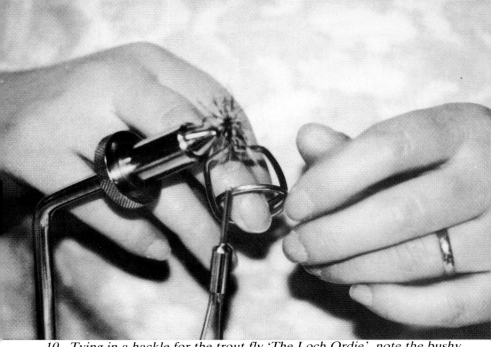

10. *Tying in a hackle for the trout fly 'The Loch Ordie', note the bushy hackle.*

CASTING SEQUENCE

11.(a) *Keep your casting technique as simple and as fluid as you can:—*
    (a) shake line out.

11.(b) 'Bring the rod smartly <u>up</u> to the perpendicular.'

11.(c) 'Pause to allow the line to flow out behind and then throw the line <u>forward</u>.'

11.(d) Note the line is going <u>out</u> above the water — it should not come down with a crash!

11.(e) The end result!

PERMITS

The cost of day permits for boat or bank fishing, on trout lochs of very good quality, is extremely reasonable, north of Inverness. Good bank fishing can be had for as little as £2-£3 for the day and boats for as little as £7-£12 per day. Given the quality of fishing and the infinite number and variety of lochs available, no one should balk at paying such a small sum for a permit.

Sources of permits and other information include local Angling Associations, Tourist Information Centres, Tackle Shops, local hotels, Estate offices and Riparian owners. If you are in a very remote area the tiny Post Offices can often supply the necessary advice and I have often found them very helpful with details of angling club secretaries names and addresses.

Where possible, in the section detailing the lochs, I have named the supplier of permits, but do remember that lochs occasionally 'change hands' and if in doubt consult the nearest tackle dealer or post office. Remember also that some hotels reserve their fishings for hotel guests, particularly boats, but sometimes bank fishing may be had on enquiry.

—— ○ ——

COMMON GAELIC NAMES FOR THE LOCHS

If you have ever wondered why some of the tongue twisting Gaelic loch names crop up time and time again here are translations of some of the most common. An interpretation of the loch name can aid your decision on whether to visit it and also what you can loosely expect to find there...

Loch A'Choire — Loch in a corrie — can be a very cold deep loch as this type are usually high in the hills in a scooped basin of rock. There will be fish there but size is debatable.

Loch A'Mhuilinn — Loch of the mill — usually of historical interest only as a few of the old water mills remain in existance.

Loch Beg — Little loch — self explanatory.

Loch Caol — Narrow loch — it may mean a very long walk round if the wind suddenly changes direction!

Loch Clach (or *Nan Clach*) — 'Stony loch' — often refers to a boulder strewn shore which makes wading very difficult however remember the rule of thumb 'Big stones equal big fish', it may be worth perservering.

Loch Crocach (or *Creagach*) — rocky loch and the same interpretation as 'Clach' applies.

Loch Dubh — Black loch — can refer to bleak surroundings or to the colour of the water itself. If it is very peaty the fish will all be small (see section on 'water').

Loch Eilein (or *Eileinach*) — Loch of islands — Always a good loch to try as the islands give added food sources for the trout and provide good holding areas.

Loch Fada — Long loch, self explanatory.

Loch Fiadhaidh — Wild loch — can refer to lack of shelter from any gales!

Loch Gainich or *Gainmhich* or similar — Sandy loch — often refers to sandy beaches around the shores, can be poor feeding for the fish if there is little weed growth, therefore the fish may be plentiful but small.

Loch Garve (or *Garbh*) — Rough loch — usually a wild and windswept loch.

Loch Glas — Grey loch — usually what all lochs look like at a distance so not really of much help!

Gorm Loch — Blue loch — could mean it is a fertile loch and worth a visit.

Loch Meadie — Narrow loch — same interpretation as 'Caol'.

Loch Mhor (or *More*) — big loch.

Loch Nam Breac — Loch of trout, at least you know there are fish present but it can sometimes mean a proliferation of small fish.

Loch Nam Breac Buidhe — Loch of Golden Trout — always worth a visit as the bigger fish are often golden bellied and deliciously pink fleshed.

Loch Na Moine — Loch of peat — usually refers to a peat bog and if the water is darkly stained the fish will usually be very small. — Wading can be very dangerous off peat hags.

Loch Nan Clachan Geala — Loch of White stones — could be limestone based and very worthwhile.

Loch Nan Eun — Green loch — could be a rich and fertile loch and well worth a visit.

Loch Poll (or *Pollain*) — Boggy loch, same interpretation as 'Na Moine'.

Loch Sgeirach (or *Skerray*) — loch of skerries — always worth going as skerries can hold some big fish off them.

THE LOCHS

CAITHNESS TROUT LOCHS

For ease of reference I have 'divided' Caithness into four areas as shown on the accompanying map on page 38-39. They fall quite neatly into various Estates or Angling Club interests so either choose your particular area or select your loch from the index if you know its name. Consult O.S. map No's 11 and 12 for detailed reading.

AREA 1 NORTH WEST CAITHNESS

This area contains moorland, forestry and 'cattle country' lochs and unless otherwise stated all the lochs contain indigenous brown trout.

Loch Calder

Permits — Harpers Fly Fishing Shop or Pentland Sports, Thurso.

This remains a favourite loch of mine in Caithness. It is easily accessible and despite its propensity to produce small fish each year I usually manage one or two in the 1½lb class. It can be easily waded along the East shore, the West side being best tackled from a boat due to its very boggy banks in places. There are car parks at the North and South ends and boats are all moored in the Southern corner. It is the only loch in Caithness which allows spinning but given the weather fish come readily enough to the fly. Best conditions are mild, cloudy and a good wind blowing and it fishes best early and late season. Highly recommended for all the family.

Flies — Butchers, Zulu, Wickhams and Pennel.

Loch Olginey

Permits — none required but consult riparian owners before crossing their land.

This is a very picturesque loch lying just to the south of Calder and fishes best in the evening in dull mild conditions. There are very fat pink fleshed trout in this loch but getting them out is a painstaking business as they are mainly bottom feeders. It is easily waded as it is very shallow but in high winds it becomes unfishable due to sediments being stirred up. The birdlife and surrounds compensate for any lack of fish and its a peaceful place to spend an evening and if you do catch one it will be into the pounds rather than ounces!

Flies — Butchers, Zulus, Wickhams and anything you have the most faith in!

—— ○ ——

Scrabster Loch

Permits — Harpers Fly Fishing Shop — Thurso.

In 1988 this loch underwent a comprehensive re-stocking programme and permits are issued for the day or the evening at very reasonable cost. Best results seem to come at night and it is a lovely peaceful loch to wade as the sun sets. The bottom is shingle and marl and the trout average ¾lb upwards. Along the partly submerged dyke is a good area to try but as it is a small loch fish rise and are taken along most of its shores. Early season is best.

Flies — Wickhams Fancy, Conemara Black and those of that ilk.

Loch Shurrery

Permits — Dounreay Fly Fishing Assoc, Mr W. Carruthers Keeper.

This is a large impressive loch at the head of the Forss River and it is dammed at its northern end. There are considerable numbers of fish in the loch but unfortunately few grow bigger than 6-7oz in weight.

Fishing on this estate is largely private and preserved and permission must be sought before starting to fish. Other lochs on the Shurrery Estate include *Loch Scye, Tuim Ghlais and Caluim* and generally speaking these are all private.

Lochs Thormaid and Saorach

Permits — Fountain Forestry, J Atkinson, 8 Sinclair Street, Thurso.

These lochs lie off the minor road leading to Shurrery Lodge South West of the town of Thurso. They can be easily reached via a forestry track. They are recommended if one has never viewed first hand the nature of commercial tree planting operations, in the Far North. The trout vary in size from a few ounces to a few much bigger.

Flies — Traditional patterns.

—— O ——

Loch Olginey

CAITHNESS and SUTHERLAND

SUTHERLAND

Area (1) NW Sutherland
Durness, Cape Wrath, Kinlochbervie, Rhiconich, Scourie and others.

Area (2) N Sutherland
Lochs at Tongue, Bettyhill, Altnaharra and others.

Area (3) N and Central Sutherland
Lochs at Melvich, Strathy, Forsinard, Kinbrace and Garvault.

Area (4) West Sutherland
Lochs at Drumbeg, Assynt, Lochinver, Elphin and Inchnadamph.

Area (5) Central Sutherland
Loch Shin, Lairg Lochs, Overscaig and Oykel Bridge lochs and others.

Area (6) SE Sutherland
Kyle of Sutherland, Dornoch, Brora, Golspie and Rogart lochs.

Cape Wrath

Durness

SUTHERLAND

DIONARD

Tongu

1

2

Scourie

Altnaharra

Inchnadamph

5

Lochinver

KIRKAIG

4

CASSLEY

Lairg

N

OYKEL

Bonar Br

KYLE OF SUTHERLAND

10 KM

— FOR DETAILED READING CONSULT OS MAP NO.s 9, 10, 11, 12, 15, 16, 17, 20, 21 of the 1: 50,000 series.

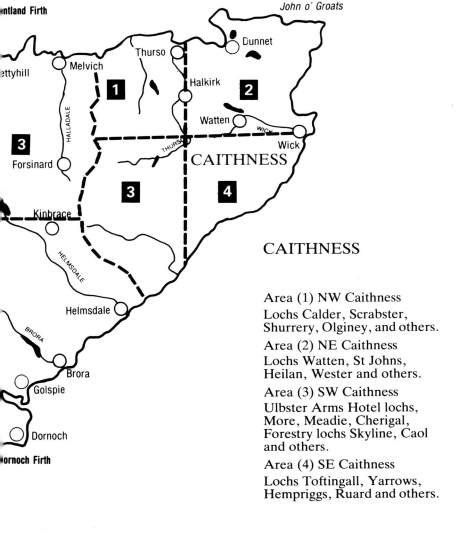

CAITHNESS

Area (1) NW Caithness
Lochs Calder, Scrabster,
Shurrery, Olginey, and others.

Area (2) NE Caithness
Lochs Watten, St Johns,
Heilan, Wester and others.

Area (3) SW Caithness
Ulbster Arms Hotel lochs,
More, Meadie, Cherigal,
Forestry lochs Skyline, Caol
and others.

Area (4) SE Caithness
Lochs Toftingall, Yarrows,
Hempriggs, Ruard and others.

AREA 2 NORTH EAST CAITHNESS

This area is mainly 'farming country' and the lochs are fertile and shallow with excellent quality trout present...

Loch Watten

Permits — Loch Watten Hotel, Watten Lodge, Harpers Fly Fishing Shop, Pentland Sports Emporium, Thurso and Hugo Ross Tackle Shop, Wick.

Many have come from far and wide to fish on Loch Watten, as it is renowned for its large, pink fleshed trout of spine tingling, fighting ability. Having said that, catches began to decline in the mid 80's, largely due, it is believed, to the loch being heavily poached with all sorts of illegal methods.

However in 1989 and 1990 there was an improvement after a slump in fish size and fish are averaging ¾-1lb up. Both boat and bank fishing are freely available and wading can be recommended in the evening around dusk as the bigger fish move in to feed. An outboard is better for the boat, as the loch is 3 miles long, and wading is best at the Eastern end where the ground is stony and firm. The water is gin clear and the bottom marl and stone, most parts of the loch are shallow with good feeding for the trout. Highly recommended early and late season and choose a cloudy, breezy day as Watten can be very dour with the slightest hint of sun!

Flies — Soldier Palmer, Wickhams Fancy, Conemara Black, Loch Ordie.

Loch Scarmclate

Permits — Riparian owners, Harpers Fly Fishing Shop, Thurso (boat).

This small loch next to Watten is picturesque and charmingly framed with trees on its northern shores. In winter there is a multitude of birdlife present and rooks nest raucously in the tall beech and elm. I would recommend boat only on this loch as the shoreline is dangerously boggy and holed in places. The fish average ¾lb or so and are of good quality.

Flies — As for Watten with addition of the Zulu.

Loch St Johns

Permits — Northern Sands Hotel Dunnet, Riparian Owners.

Circular St John's Loch is a well maintained high quality fishery with its own association "St John's Loch Improvement Assoc". It is a shallow loch with good feeding and some very large trout of the pink fleshed variety. In high winds the loch has a tendency to sediment up making it unfishable so try and visit during a calmish spell. There is a hatch of mayfly in June and fish up to 2lb or so can be taken at that time. It is highly recommended with both boat and bank fishing available. Off the bank is a bit muddy here and there but worth having a go late in the evening.

Prepare the glass case just in case! — Wheelie boat facilities for the disabled.

Flies:— Wickhams, Invicta, Soldier Palmer, Black pennel. A dry fly can work wonders on a cloudy summer evening.

Dunnet Head Lochs

Permits:— Brough Tea Room, Dunnet Head.

These are an interesting group of small hill lochs off the minor road leading to Dunnet Head lighthouse. They are the most northerly lochs in Britain and have a good Association, 'Dunnet Head Fishing Club' formed in 1980. Fishing is all from the bank with a size limit of 10 inches and the Club stock the lochs. The water is peaty and acidic and the lochs gained the reputation for small fish, but since the Club was formed with its restocking policy fish sizes have improved and fish up to 2lb are sometimes taken on these rough moorland lochs. The Black Loch and the 'Many Loch' chain produce the best fish and they make a pleasant change if nearby neighbour St John's is proving too difficult.

Flies:— Zulu, Pennel, Bibio etc.

Loch Heilan

Permits:— Mr Pottinger, Greenlands Farm.

This is probably the most difficult water in Caithness. Set in a fertile basin on farmland it is a shallow loch with clear water and a prolific yellow algae growth. The bottom is pale mud, marl and stones and the fish are bottom feeders growing to an excellent size — in 1988 a fish of 8lbs was recorded! Having said that I would not rush for the glass case as they are exceedingly difficult to catch. Most locals fish the loch in the evening when you may just tempt a fish from its lie. Boat and bank fishing is available and good wading can be had off the stonier ground of the North and South shores. Recommended for those who want a very serious challenge but do not be surprised if you have blank days.

Flies:— Soldier Palmer worked for me once (I lost the fish!) otherwise use what you put the most faith in!

Loch of Wester

Permits:— Harpers Fly Fishing Shop, Thurso and Auckhorn Farm

This is the only loch in Caithness famed for its seatrout rather than its browns. It is also open to October 31st while most of the other lochs close on October 6th. This is to allow for a good seatrout 'run'. Boat and bank fishing and wading is all from the North shore. Choose a cloudy day and watch out for some spectacular fish with seatrout up to 3lb being recorded. Highly recommended for 'back end' fishing.

Flies:— Butchers, Silver Invicta, Dunkeld, Wickhams, Peter Ross and any of your favourite sea trout flies.

AREA 3 SOUTH WEST CAITHNESS

This area of Caithness encompasses the Loch Dubh Estate moorland fishings and the Fountain Forestry Lochs in the Altnabreac area...

Loch Caol

Permits:— Fountain Forestry, J Atkinson, Sinclair Street, Thurso.

A narrow loch to the North East of Altnabreac station. It contains good quality trout with boat and bank fishing available. The fish average ¾lb or so.

Flies:— Traditional patterns.

Loch Caise

Permits:— Fountain Forestry

Caise is directly south of the Caol loch over the railway line and can be reached via the rough track leading east from Altnabreac station. It contains smaller trout than Caol but they are very free rising.

Flies:— Traditional Patterns.

Loch Garbh

Permits:— Fountain Forestry.

Garbh lies to the East of Caise and contains excellent trout averaging ¾lb upwards. The loch is easily waded with a bottom of shingle and sand and the fish are pink fleshed and delicious.

Flies:— Traditional patterns.

Loch Beul Na Faire (Skyline)

Permits:— Fountain Forestry

Between Caol loch and Altnabreac station slightly west of Caol, lies the small narrow Skyline loch. This loch gained a good reputation for large fish some years ago and it still has though they are getting harder to catch. Excellent trout averaging 1lb up and of the pink fleshed variety.

Flies:— Traditional patterns.

Authors Note — All the Fountain Forestry lochs can be reached (more or less) by a network of forestry roads not shown on old O/S maps. It is important to obtain permits, directions and keys for gates before setting out and do remember that a high wheel based vehicle is advised on most of the tracks.

Loch More

Permits:— Ulbster Arms Hotel, Halkirk.

This is the largest loch on the Loch Dubh Estate. At one time it was fished mainly for salmon as it forms part of the length of the River Thurso. Todays anglers are concerned with the trout however, which average ½lb or so, though it is still possible to catch a rare salmon or two so be prepared. Sandy bays and good promontories and reasonable wading with care. Can be bleak however and easily become wave lashed and windswept with little or no shelter in a gale so choose your day if you can! Boat and bank fishing available.

Flies:— Traditional Patterns.

Loch a' Cherigal

Permits:— Ulbster Arms Hotel.

Cherigal is set to the north of Strathmore lodge in peaty moorland. Watch how you choose your path to it and follow the white posts provided. Not the place for big baskets but some very big trout lurk in the depths of this one. Fish up to 2-3lb are quite common. Can be a bit dour and frustrating but persevere, one for the glass case may just be awaiting you! The promontory on the East side is a good holding area and wading is reasonable. Boat and bank fishing.

Flies:— Wickhams, Zulu, Pennel etc.

Loch Meadie

Permits:- Ulbster Arms Hotel.

Meadie is the narrow loch to the west of Cherigal easily reached from the Strathmore lodge road. The fish are not as big as Cherigals but can give good sport averaging ½lb up. Little or no shelter in a gale but pleasant enough for a days trouting. Boat and bank fishing.

Flies:— Traditional patterns.

Loch Eileanach

Permits:— Ulbster Arms Hotel.

West of Meadie lies Eileanach and the lochs are of similar size and shape and size of fish is roughly the same averaging ½lb or so. Boat and bank fishing.

Flies:— Traditional patterns.

Loch Dubh Nan Geo

Permits:— Ulbster Arms Hotel.

This loch lies to the west of Eileanach and is not one of the better known Ulbster Arms waters. However historically it has received some press with some large trout of the 5-6lb class being taken off it. It has some good promontories and bays — could be interesting!

Flies:— Traditional patterns.

Loch Gaineimh

Permits:— Ulbster Arms Hotel

A loch full of small free rising trout and ideal for the beginner. It is often the scene of junior angling competitions.

Flies:— Traditional patterns.

Loch A Mhuillinn

Permits:— Ulbster Arms Hotel.

High wheel based vehicles are a distinct advantage for reaching this loch. Go down the west bank of Loch More to Dalnawillan lodge and then across the moor as if making for Altanabreac Station. The loch is right by the track and contains strong fish of ½lb upwards.

Flies:— Traditional patterns.

Loch Dubh

Permits:— Ulbster Arms Hotel.

The main attraction of the loch is the imposing spires of the Loch Dhu Hotel adjacent to the loch, a monument to a past hunting/shooting/fishing age. The building was bought over in 1988 so enquire at the Ulbster Arms about angling rights.

Loch Eun and Rumsdale

Permits:— Ulbster Arms Hotel.

South west of Altnabreac station along the bumpy track are these grand little lochs and both hold fish of superb quality with the average weight 1lb upwards. Excellent fishing and highly recommended.

Flies:— Traditional patterns.

Loch Airigh Leathaid

Permits:— Ulbster Arms Hotel.

Far into the wilds past the Dalnawhillan Lodge and south west of 'Dalganachan', below an area known imposingly as the 'Craggan' lie these excellent lochs, illustrious 'neighbours' of Eun and Rumsdale and the fish are of similar size and quality. Good wading and highly recommended if you like your fishing serene and remote.

Flies:— Traditional patterns.

Loch Glutt

Permits:— Ulbster Arms Hotel

Even further out at Glutt Lodge lies this small shear sided loch. Fish of 3-4lb are not uncommon in this one and if you can make the effort to get there you may be rewarded by a large fish or two.

Flies:— Traditional patterns.

Loch Thulachan and Sand

Permits:— Ulbster Arms Hotel.

Lying to the south east of Loch More these lochs entail a good walk across the moor and are recommended for those enjoying invigorating exercise prior to fishing. Both contain free rising trout averaging ½lb or so. The Thulachan house is imposing above the two lochs and considerable effort must have gone into its building in such a remote area.

Flies:— Traditional patterns.

—— ○ ——

AREA 4 SOUTH EAST CAITHNESS

In area 4 the lochs are not so numerous but that does not detract from their quality and they are mainly set in moorland terrain.

Loch Toftingall

Permits:— Fountain Forestry

This loch has recently been the centre of some heated controversy over the conifer planting going on near the water — some have argued the loch has been sedimented up from the industrial ploughing methods of the forestry and others have argued it is prone to sedimentation anyway with high winds. At the time of writing it was still producing reasonable fish in the ¾lb class and there is a bag limit of 10 fish in force. Boat and bank fishing though parts of the bank are boggy so take care. A forestry road runs right to the boat house.

Flies:— Traditional patterns.

Loch Stemster

Permits:— Latheron Wheel Estate.

This is a very attractive, almost circular loch off the A895 to Latheron near the Rumster forest. There are a number of good promontories and bays and both boat and bank fishing are available. It contains good fish in the ½-1lb range and the Standing Stones catch the eye to the south of the loch. The southern end is a good area to try first but fish can be caught all round the loch. Highly recommended for a visit.

Flies:— Traditional patterns.

Loch Hempriggs

Permits:— Thrumster Filling Station, Thrumster, Wick.

This is a reasonable sized loch lying adjacent to the main A9 between Wick and Thrumster. The fish are in the ½-¾lb range and give good account of themselves. Can be a windswept loch but boat and bank fishing are available. Wading requires a bit of care but can be undertaken.

Flies:— Traditional patterns.

Loch Sarclet

Permits:— Thrumster Filling Station, Thrumster, Wick.

This loch is very popular with model yacht enthusiasts. The fishing can be very dour and the loch can become weedy near the end of the season. The fish in the past have been averaging ¾lb or so but it is a difficult business getting them out.

Flies:— Traditional patterns.

Loch of Yarrows

Permits:— Thrumster Filling station, Thrumster, Wick.

A picturesque loch surrounded by gentle hills. It is deep and full of small free rising trout. Boat and bank fishing available. The most interesting part of this loch is its 'extension' along the road. Here the fish have grown fat on flooded farmland and this part comes highly recommended with fish up to 2lb being taken. — It is not on any of the older OS maps but it is definitely there and well worth a cast.

Flies:— Soldier Palmer, Invicta, Pennel etc.

Loch Ruard and Rangag

Permits:— Latheron Wheel Estate.

Rangag is right by the road virtually opposite Loch Stemster. A bleak loch it contains small free rising trout. Ruard is much further out to the north west of Rangag and contains good fish averaging ½lb for those willing to walk out — its a fair haul over the rough moor!

Flies:— Traditional patterns.

—— O ——

SUTHERLAND TROUT LOCHS

Sutherland is by far the bigger of the two Counties and thus I have had to divide it into 6 sections (maps p38-39), so as to encompass all the various Estates and Angling Club waters. There are also considerably more lochs here and several of the descriptions have had to be 'collective' rather than 'individual'. However all the lochs of Sutherland contain native wild brown trout ranging from a few ounces to many pounds in weight and it is perhaps my favourite county in Scotland for its diverse, challenging and remote fishings... For detailed reading consult OS map numbers 9, 10, 11, 15, 16 and 17.

AREA 1 NORTH WEST SUTHERLAND

This area encompasses Durness, Cape Wrath, Kinlochbervie and Scourie.

Limestone Lochs of Durness

These exquisite trout lochs are a must for the serious angler. I cannot recommend them too highly, and though my visits to them are all too rare, they remain my favourite lochs in Sutherland. Even just writing about them makes me want to pack the rod and head out West! They number...

Loch Borralie

Permits:— Cape Wrath Hotel

Nestling to the rear of the Cape Wrath Hotel is this gin clear aquamarine blue trout loch of remarkable quality. The fish are excellent, beautifully marked and silver flanked, more like land locked sea-trout in fact. They average 1½lb which gives you some idea of their growth rate and please RETURN anything under a pound. The area around the island and on the opposite shore is the most productive, and the fish take your breath away! Boat and bank fishing available.

Flies:— Wickhams, Soldier Palmer, Invicta and a dry 'Daddy' on a still evening can bring an explosive response.

Loch Croispol

Permits:— Cape Wrath Hotel.

Another top quality water with fish averaging a pound upwards. The first time I saw this loch I thought I was looking at sea water, such is its ice blue clarity! The fish are again beautifully marked and boat and bank fishing are available. If wading keep to the West shore as elsewhere is preserved. Highly recommended.

Flies:— Same as Borralie.

Loch Caladail

Permits:— Cape Wrath Hotel.

The fish here are more golden than their Borralie 'neighbours' but grow just as big and strong with fish in the 3 - 4lb class taken regularly. Boat and bank fishing and please return any 'small' fish under a pound. There are leviathans to be had, so it is better for all to do so. Highly recommended.

Flies:— Zulu, Pennel, Wickhams etc.

Loch Lanlish

Permits:— Cape Wrath Hotel.

This tiny sandy loch holds the biggest fish of all the Durness lochs but it also the most difficult. Pictures in the hotel show the size of fish which can be taken from it (in the 7-8 lb class and the average is 4 lb or so!) — Very dour and I wish you luck, its always worth a try!

Flies:— Your selection!

Cape Wrath Trout Lochs

Permits:— Cape Wrath Hotel.

The Cape Wrath peninsula is stunningly beautiful and remote and a visit to the lighthouse and its towering cliffs is a must if in the area. Take a ferry from opposite the Cape Wrath Hotel and a minibus meets you (in summer) and takes you along the only road to the lighthouse. The lochs of Cape Wrath are beautifully isolated and peaceful and are ideal for the hillwalker/loch enthusiast as some entail a good walk to reach them. A word of CAUTION — the MOD use parts of the area as a BOMBING range so always read and check MOD notices prior to crossing and BEWARE of the area marked DANGER on O.S. maps — unexploded shells are present and the area is extremely hazardous.

The lochs include:—

Inshore, Keisgaig, Bad an Fheur, Airigh na Beinne, Gammhich and others. All hold stocks of hard fighting trout and are lightly fished for obvious reasons! They average ½lb or so with the possibility of bigger fish on the odd occasion. Take stout footwear, light tackle, map and compass and enjoy the wilderness, but do follow routes as designated by the issuers of the permit.

Flies:— Traditional patterns.

Kinlochbervie Lochs

Permits:— Enquire at the local Post Office as these lochs appear to be on an estate believed to be known as the Oldshoremore Estate and some are up for sale at the time of writing.

12. *A tempting ripple on loch Meadie, Loch Dubh Estate, Caithness. A typical moorland loch with Ben Dorrery visible to the North.*

13. *The vast wilderness of Sutherland can take on an almost dream like quality as in this unusual shot of Altnaharras' Loch Meadie to the rear of Ben Loyal.*

14. *Autumn sunset and west winds over Loch Calder, Caithness.*

15. The almost infinate horizon of the central region of Sutherland looking out over Loch a Ghorm and Loch Faig near Lairg.

16. A storm and a glint of sun highlight the rugged terrain around Loch Coulside, the small loch to the South West of Loch Loyal, North Sutherland.

17. *Early season prospects are usually very good on a warm April day like this at Loch Calder, Caithness.*

18. *The peak of Ben Stack rises prominently above the end of Loch More, North West Sutherland. Beyond this the Scourie wilderness awaits.*

19. The tranquility of fishing in the Far North. The Lily Loch and Loch Hakel, Tongue, Sutherland. Ben Hope rising up into the clouds to the South.

20. The author wading around the skerries on Loch Hakel, Tongue, North Sutherland.

21. *The Loch Dhu Hotel now sadly disused, stands as a proud monument to a bygone hunting/shooting/fishing age. (Loch Dhu itself is the water in the foreground.)*

22. *Loch an t-Seilge high in the hills of Central Sutherland, Reay Forest.*

23. *Wild trout from Loch Na Caorach, Sutherland.*

24. *The Author, Lesley Crawford, ready for the Lochs.*

Although these lochs are not well known they do have in their number the very impressive *Sandwood loch* situated next to the marvellously isolated beaches of Sandwood bay. You may have to leave the rod in the car for this one, but the walk out is invigorating and the scenery marvellous. There is a rough track to take the car along part of the way and off it lie a number of attractive hill lochs including *Loch Na Gainimh*, *Loch a`Mhuilinn* and *Loch Mor a`Chraisg*. They appear to be of similar quality to the Cape Wrath (northern half) hill lochs.

The whole area is dramatic and remote and worth a visit even if angling is unavailable. Choose a good day and take the camera!

Flies:— Traditional patterns.

Rhiconich Estate and Hotel lochs

The Estate has a number of trout lochs available for the guests and most of these are very good quality fishings. Enquiries should be made directly to the Manager. The lochs are mostly in the Rhiconich and Oldshoremore area and the scenery is grand and remote with the quartzite tops of Foinaven and Arkle to the South East. Day permits are available through the Estate office at Inshegra, and at the Rhiconich Hotel.

Scourie hill Lochs

Permits:— Scourie Angling Club, Scourie Hotel and other hotels in the area.

To the visiting angler Scourie represents a small 'Nirvana' — round every corner, another new water appears, and the whole area is pitted with lochs, large and small, by the road, or lost in the hills. A conservative estimate of the number of lochs in the Scourie area would be 300 or so and all contain brown trout of various sizes! — I personally found this quantity of lochs almost unnerving, and spent considerable time dithering about which one to try next, there was so much good trouting water on offer!

For this area I really must advise joining the Scourie Angling Club and getting first hand local knowledge of which lochs are fishing best and/or staying at one of the excellent fishing hotels there — they have more waters available than you could fish in a lifetime!

Flies:— All the traditional patterns.

Authors Note:—

The large lochs of *Stack*, *More* and *Hope* in Area 1 are primarily concerned with excellent salmon and sea-trout fishing and not really of interest to the brown trout enthusiast. However if these fish are your determined quarry for Stack and More try the Westminster Estates Office at Achfary and for Hope, the Altnaharra Hotel and riparian owners, Keepers House, North End.

AREA 2 NORTH SUTHERLAND

This area encompasses some of my 'home' territory of Tongue, Bettyhill and Altnaharra and the fishings are mainly administered through the Tongue and District Angling Club and the local hotels.

Loch Loyal

Permits:— Tongue and District Angling Club, Tongue Hotel, Ben Loyal Hotel and others.

The largest loch in the area holding some really marvellous fish, this water is to be highly recommended. The fish start about ¾lb and some really large fish in the 3-5lb class are recorded every year. They are frighteningly strong, silver flanked and pink fleshed and Loyal fish on their day, can give you the thrill of a lifetime! Boat and bank fishing available and wading is good with shingle and sand beaches and promontories here and there to assist casting. The southern shores produce some giants but fish can be taken from all round the loch. It fishes best early and late in the season and the water is sparklingly clear.

Flies:— Wickhams, Soldier Palmer, Conemara Black, and Nymphs for early season work.

Ben Loyal over Loch Hakel.

50

Loch Hakel (Hacoin)

Permits:— Tongue and District Angling Club and local hotels.

This is one of my favourite small lochs in Sutherland nestling as it does at the foot of Ben Loyal. The scenery around it is matchless and the fish are well up to their dramatic surroundings averaging ¾lb or so, strong and pink fleshed. Boat and bank fishing and wading is good near the islands and skerries where the bigger fish lie. A superb loch.

Flies:— Kingfisher Butcher, Soldier Palmer, Zulu, Silver Invicta.

Loch Modsarie, Skerray, Tigh Choimhid, A' Chaoruinn, Cormaic and Nam Breac Buidhe

Permits:— Tongue and District Angling Club.

These lochs are all in the Borgie Forest area and are again highly recommended for those who like quality fishing in stunning surroundings. *Nam Breac Buidhe* holds the largest fish but is also the most difficult to fish. *Cormaic* is nearest to Tongue situated to the rear of Dalcharn farm while the other lochs lie off the Skerray ring road. *Loch Skerray* itself holds the best fish of this group but all can produce quality trout averaging ½lb upwards with much larger fish in the 2-3lb class taken occasionally. Peaceful and remote and well worth visiting.

Flies:— Wickhams, Pennels, Loch Ordie on a windy day.

Lochs Bhuldaidh, Na' H-airigh Bige, Fhionnaich and a 'Mhuillin, Lily Loch.

Permits:— Tongue and District Angling Club, local hotels.

These hill lochs lie to the west of Tongue in the Kinloch and Melness area. Again they are all highly recommended though some entail a good walk to get there. Good quality trout averaging ½lb up with some much larger fish taken from time to time.

Flies:— As for *Lochs Modsarie* etc.

Loch An Dherue (pronunced Loch Veroo) also known as Loch An Deerie

This large loch lies south of Kinloch Lodge and is primarily concerned with salmon and sea-trout, and is privately owned at the time of writing.

Lochs Craggie and Sliam

Permits:— Tongue Hotel, Ben Loyal Hotel, Tongue and District A/C for Craggie.

These are two lochs to the North of Loch Loyal and as they are the head waters of the Borgie River it is possible to catch a salmon in them after a spate and a run of fish. The trout are of reasonable quality averaging ½-¾lb and fight well.

Flies:— Traditional patterns.

Bettyhill Hotel Fishings

Permits:— Bettyhill Hotel.

The Bettyhill Hotel has a number of trout lochs available for guests and enquiry for fishing these lochs should be made directly to the Manager. They number in their midsts lochs *Meadie, Mor, Caol, Airigh Na Creige* amongst others. All hold good trout averaging ½lb upwards and are set in splendid moorland scenery.

Flies:— Traditional patterns.

Altnaharra Hotel Fishings

Permits:— Altnaharra Hotel.

This area to the south of Tongue via the A836 or the B871 has some excellent trout lochs on offer. The hotel reserves fishing for its guests but the visiting angler is usually accommodated if possible. The lochs available include *Loch Naver* (essentially a salmon loch at the foot of Ben Klibreck), *Loch Meadie, Loch Eileanach, Loch Staink. Plantation Loch, Bad Na Gallaig, Achaidh Mhoir, Breac Buidhe* and *Tarvie*. All the lochs are highly recommended and the fish are of good size and quality.

Flies:— Traditional patterns.

—— ○ ——

AREA 3 NORTH AND CENTRAL SUTHERLAND

This area encompasses Strathy, Melvich, Forsinard, the 'Badenlochs' and the lochs of the Langwell Estate, Berriedale. The lochs are mainly administered by Fountain Forestry, the Garvault Hotel, the Melvich Hotel, the Langwell Estate Office and R. McNicol, Kinbrace, for Leverhulme Estates.

Strathy Hill Lochs

Most of the area south of Strathy village has now been afforested. Fountain Forestry own the land and the lochs and fishing is on the whole private. However if you wish to enquire further try Fountain Forestry (Mrs Atkinson, 8 Sinclair Street, Thurso) or the keeper resident on the Strathy Estate. The lochs can be reached via a system of forestry roads and a high wheel based vehicle is desirable. The lochs include *Nan Clach, Meala* and *Buidhe* and they hold excellent fish for those who do not mind their fishings 'tree-lined'.

Flies:— Traditional patterns.

Melvich hill lochs

Permits:— Melvich Hotel

In recent years the fishing rights for these lochs have been 'to-ing and fro-ing' between Fountain Forestry and the Melvich Hotel and at the time of writing the hotel has once again secured permits. The lochs are on either side of the Strath Halladale road on the high rough moor and some entail a very long arduous walk to get there. The area has not been afforested however, so at present the lochs retain their moorland character and are well worth a visit. They include . . . .

Loch Na Caorach, Akran, Caol and na Seilge

Permits:— Melvich Hotel

These lie to the East of the Strath Halladale Road about 2 miles down from the Melvich end. There is a track leading up the hillside near the electricity pylons and this leads you out on to the moor. *Na Caorach* is first, narrow and peaty but holding some good fish averaging ¾lb or so. Going east, *Na Seilge* (*'Shallag'* to the locals) holds some good trout and is clearer watered with bouldered shores. Boat and bank fishing. *Caol* and *Akran* lie directly to the north of *Na Seilge* and have smaller fish but are pleasant for a day out on the moors away from it all with big baskets frequently taken.

Flies:— Zulu, Invicta, Wickhams.

Lochs Eaglaise Mor and Eaglaise Beag

Permits:— Melvich Hotel

These lochs lie to the west of the Strath Halladale road and both entail a long walk to get there. They can be approached either from the north down one of the tracks and across the moor or from the east again along one of the stoney tracks and over the heath. Take a map and compass in case the mist descends and wear stout footwear it can be very boggy! — Many locals make the effort to get there however, and justly so because the fishing is excellent quality and the fish average ¾lb up with fish in the 1-2lb class taken frequently. Good wading and highly recommended.

Flies:— Wickhams, Pennel, Zulu, Butcher.

Loch Earach

Permits:— Melvich Hotel per Mr Murray.

A tiny stocked loch right by the A897. Wading only but pleasant enough for a few hours casting.

Flies:— Traditional patterns.

Forsinard Hotel Fishings

Permits:— Forsinard Hotel.

This hotel has a number of good trout lochs available mainly for guests and enquiry should be made directly to the manager. Another heavily afforested area, and the lochs can be reached by the ubiquitous forestry roads which run between the conifer plantations. The lochs include *Sletill, Leir, Talaheel, Nam Breac, Cross lochs* and others. The fish average ½-¾lb with a few larger fish taken, up to 1½lb, from time to time.

Flies:— Traditional patterns.

Badenloch System (Loch Rimsdale and others)

Permits:— Garvault Hotel, Leverhulme Estate, Kinbrace. Factor, Langwell Estate Berriedale.

There are a fair number of lochs in this system and they are well known for good quality trouting in striking moorland surroundings. They number . . . .

Loch Rimsdale, Nan Clar, Badenloch

Permits:— Garvault Hotel, Leverhulme Estate, Kinbrace.

These lochs are the largest in the area and are interconnecting. Situated to the south of the Garvault Hotel they appear as a vast watery plain with sandy bays, skerries and small islands. There are Forestry Commission plantations of mature trees on the north and west side and the whole vista is one of open moorland, with the hills of Armine and Klibreck to the south. Boat and bank fishing available but a boat is recommended to cover such a lot of water successfully. The trout average ½lb up and the occasional salmon is also taken.

Flies:— Traditional patterns.

Loch An Ruathair, Arichlinie, Culiadh, Lucy, Druim a Chiabhain and Coire Nam Mang.

Permits:— Langwell Estate Office, Berriedale, and Leverhulme Estate, Kinbrace.

An Ruathair is right by the Strath Halladale road south of Forsinard and holds considerable numbers of bright smallish fish of ½lb or so. Arichlinie, Culiadh, and Lucy are all in its vicinity holding similar quality of fish and the scenery is splendid with the Ben Griam's dominating the skyline. Loch Druim a' Chliabhain (also called Leum a Chlamhain) lies between the two hills and holds excellent trout averaging ¾lb up. It is quite a walk to it and it is best approached from near the rear of the Garvault Hotel but it is well worth the effort and this one comes highly recommended as does its smaller 'sister' loch Coire Nam Mang.

Flies:— Traditional patterns.

Lochs Fearna, Truderscaig

Permits:— Garvault Hotel, Loch Choire Estate, Leverhulme Estate.

An Fearna lies off the track south of the Loch Badenloch leading into Loch Choire Lodge at the foot of Ben Armine and Truderscaig can also be reached from the same track. Again good quality trouting waters in delightful scenery.

Flies:— Traditional patterns.

AREA 4 WEST SUTHERLAND

This area encompasses another rich myriad of trouting waters with the principal areas of interest being Drumbeg, Stoer, Lochinver, Assynt, Inchnadamph and Elphin.

Drumbeg Fishings

Permits:— Drumbeg Hotel, riparian owners.

The road to Drumbeg village is one of the most narrow and tortuous routes I have ever had the pleasure to drive on so approach with some caution — we ended up in a ditch once! It is worth making the journey however as the trout lochs are of good quality and the scenery quite magnificent. The mountain 'Quinag' stands sentinal to the east of most of the lochs and it should be noted that some of the lochs require a fair walk to reach them. Principal lochs of interest include *Loch Drumbeg, The Gorm Lochs Mor* and *Beag, Loch Fada, Loch Skerrach, Loch Tolla Bhaid* and *Loch na loinne*. Fishing may be solely reserved for guests at the height of the season but the visiting angler can usually be accommodated somewhere. Boat and bank fishing on most of the waters.

Flies:— Traditional patterns.

Assynt Angling Club Lochs (Stoer, Lochinver and Inverkirkaig areas)

Permits:— Tourist Information Centre, Lochinver hotels.

There are 34 lochs on offer from this excellent angling Association. They offer good quality trouting with fish averaging ½lb upwards with the occasional larger fish caught not infrequently so check the knots before casting! The club produce a booklet complete with maps indicating all the lochs available and they range from roadside to very remote. Fishing is on the whole from the bank but this does not detract in any way and the scenery around Lochinver with the sugar loafed Suilven towering above the waters is quite breathtaking. A lovely area and some of my favourite waters include:—

Loch Cul Fraoich (Stoer)

Permits — Assynt Angling Club.

This loch lies north of the hamlet of Raffin and is easily reached along a track leading in from Culkein. It is known locally as very dour but if you take a trout it could be a heavy one as fish up to 3lb have been caught in the past. Hard fishing but worth it if you enjoy a challenge.

Flies:— Your selection!

Baddidarach Hill lochs

Permits:— Assynt Angling Club.

These charming little lochs north of Lochinver are as memorable for their view of Suilven as they are the fishing. Drive out to Baddidarach and a good track leads off to the various lochs. Remote and peaceful with fish averaging ½lb or so, small but they fight like mad!

Flies:— Traditional patterns.

Loch A'Choin and Loch An Arbhair

Permits:— Assynt Angling Club.

Next to one another and known locally as the *Dog* and *Cat Loch* these ones are adjacent to the road just south of Inverkirkaig. Easily accessible they are ideal for an evenings cast. Fish average ½lb or so.

Flies:— Traditional patterns.

Lochs Beannach, Bad Nan Aighean, uidh na Geadaig

Permits:— Assynt Angling Club.

These lochs are all just to the north of the A837 between Lochinver and Little Assynt. the trout average ½-¾lb and the lochs are all very picturesque with many islands and promontaries and well worth visiting.

Flies:— Traditional Patterns.

Authors Note:—

— It should be noted that at the time of writing the Vestay Estate on which most of the Assynt lochs are situated was up for sale — let us hope these fine lochs are not lost to the visiting angler, if it does 'change hands'.

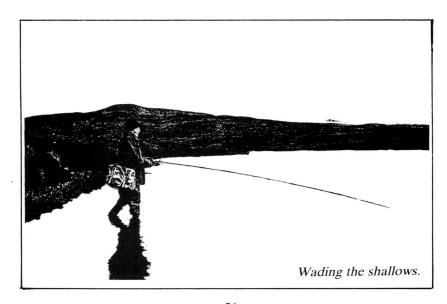

Wading the shallows.

Inchnadamph Hotel Fishings

Permits:— Inchnadamph Hotel.

The primary loch associated with this hotel is the large *Loch Assynt* with the striking ruin of Ardvreck Castle on its shores. The trout are of good quality averaging ½lb up and some very large trout come off this loch every year along with the occasional salmon. Boat and bank fishing available though because of the presence of salmon it can be more expensive. There are also a number of good hill lochs available including the *Gillaroo Loch* (so called because of the introduction of this Irish fish some years ago) and *Loch Awe* adjacent to the A837. Both are good lochs with trout averaging ¾lb up. The Hotel can also arrange fishing on *Lochs Cam* and *Veyatie* at Ledmore Junction and these are again excellent waters with Suilven prominent behind. — Note in the Inchnadamph area pockets of limestone exist giving rise to fertile lochs and some large fish.

Flies:— Traditional patterns.

Inver Lodge Fishings

Permits:— Inver Lodge Hotel (Lochinver).

This hotel 'replaced' the Culag Hotel which was shut down. It has a number of good lochs primarily reserved for its guests. They include *Loch Culag, Fionn Loch, Loch Druim Suardalain* and *Loch Veyatie* amongst others and enquiries should be made direct to the manager.

Flies:— Traditional patterns.

Altnacealgach Motel Fishings, near Elphin.

Permits:— Alncealgach Motel (bar).

This motel has 'risen from the ashes' of the old Altnacealgach Hotel which burnt down in the mid 80's. At the time of writing there is a small bar there 'The Alt Bar' but work is under way to construct an accommodation complex next to it. The motel has the rights on *Loch Borralan* directly in front of it and used to issue permits for *Lochs Cam, Veyatie* and *Urigill*. All are good trouting waters and fish average ½-¾lb upward with the larger fish being taken mainly in the evening. *Urigill* and *Borralan* are shallow lochs with good wading and some heavy fish present, Veyatie and Cam are deeper lochs with ferox also present in their depths.

Flies:— Traditional patterns.

—— O ——

AREA 5 CENTRAL SUTHERLAND

This area covers the massive Loch Shin (Lairg Angling Club) as well as the Oykel Bridge lochs, Overscaig Hotel and the Sutherland Arms Hotel lochs. It is a less mountainous area than the west coast and the Forestry Commission have some large plantations in the area, as do Fountain Forestry.

Loch Shin

Permits:— Lairg Angling Club and local hotels.

It is appropriate to start this area with its largest loch, and indeed this very large water covers most of central Sutherland! The A838 from Lairg to Rhiconich runs along all of its northern shores giving easy access for bank fishing but to cover the loch successfully one really requires a boat. These are freely available through Lairg Angling Club and the local hotels. It is a loch for those enjoying vast watery expanses with the best areas being most of the bays and the shallower north end. The south end is dammed and very deep. The fish are free risers and average ¾lb to 2lb with much larger taken now and again. The club also have a boat available on Loch Beannach.

Flies:— Traditional patterns.

Overscaig Hotel Fishings

Permits:— Overscaig Hotel.

Apart from Loch Shin this hotel also has some excellent moorland lochs including *Loch Fiag, Merkland* and *Loch a' Ghriama*. Historically Fiag contains some very large trout and round the islands would be a good place to try for them. Trout of 3-4lbs were quite common in the 20's and 30's so you never know what may be around the next corner! Merkland and a' Ghriama have trout in the ¾-1lb plus range and both are easily accessible from the A838 to Rhiconich from Lairg. Aesthetically both lochs are long and narrow but Merkland has I feel lost some of its charm from the introduction of fish cages.

Flies:— Traditional patterns.

Oykel Bridge Hotel Lochs

Permits:— Oykel Bridge Hotel.

The Hotel has a number of hill lochs available for guests including the little *Loch Craggie* adjacent to the A837. This delightful small loch holds trout in the ½-¾lb range and is clear and easily waded. Very pleasant for a few hours casting off the bank and day permits can usually be had from the hotel. The hotel also had *Loch Ailsh* at one time though it now seems to be fished by guests of the Inver Lodge hotel, Lochinver. Check with the Manager — Loch Ailsh also contains salmon and sea-trout as it is the head water of the River Oykel, and therefore would be more expensive than the brown trout waters.

Flies:— Traditional patterns.

Sutherland Arms Hotel (Lairg fishings)

Permits:— Sutherland Arms Hotel

This hotel issues permits for the hill lochs to the north of Lairg. *Lochs Beannach* and *Craggie* are probably the best known and both are worth visiting with fish averaging ¾lb up. *Loch Dola* and *Tigh na creige* are other smaller lochs in the vicinity and they are all peaceful lochs, with the large Dalchork wood to the east. The trout average around ¾lb with the heaviest trout to be found in Craggie.

Flies:— Traditional patterns.

—— ○ ——

AREA 6 SOUTH EAST SUTHERLAND

Back to the 'seaside' again for the coastal districts of Brora, Golspie, Dornoch and the Kyle of Sutherland.

Kyle of Sutherland Angling Club

Permits:— Bonar Bridge Tourist Information Centre, local shops and hotels.

This Angling Club is better known for its sea-trout fishing in the estuary of the Kyle of Sutherland and the Dornoch Firth and it is to be recommended if one wishes a change from the brown trout. However it also has *Loch Migdale* to the east of Bonar Bridge if the sea-trout are being unco-operative and this is a pleasant narrow loch holding fish of ½lb or so with boat and bank fishing available. Other club lochs include *Craical, Laro* and *Laggan*.

Flies:— Traditional patterns.

Dornoch Angling Club

Permits:— Mr W McDonald (Ironmongers), Castle Street, Dornoch.

This well run association has six lochs available to the visitor and the area though not as rugged as the west coast, is green and scenic and if the fish are not moving there is always the excellent golf course! The lochs include *Buidhe, An Lagain, Nan Laogh* and *Laro* and are all situated to the west of Dornoch on the moors. The fish vary in size and some of the lochs entail a fair walk. An ideal place for combining a golfing, fishing holiday. Boat and bank fishing available.

Flies:— Traditional patterns.

Loch Brora

Permits:— Dornoch Angling Club, Rob Wilson's Tackle Shop, Brora, Loch Brora Angling Club and numerous hotels.

This loch is primarily salmon and sea-trout and is etched in my memory as my father took me out on a boat on it, at the tender age of nine. — It was freezing and I did not catch a thing, however, the experience did nothing to dampen my enthusiasm! Nowadays things are much more expensive for the pursuit of the 'big fish', but if you have the money and the time it is a good loch to try your hand.

Flies:— Your salmon and sea-trout selection.

Golspie Angling Club Lochs

Permits:— Golspie Angling Club, Lindsay and Co, Main Street, Golspie.

Another well run angling Association with permits for *Loch Brora* (already mentioned), *Loch Lundie, Loch Horn* and *Loch Farlary. Lundie* and *Horn* contain the best fish though both involve a good walk they are worth it with fish averaging ¾lb upwards. Boat and bank fishing available. *Loch Farlary* lies in the Dunrobin glen right by the road and although the fish are smaller it is worth a cast or two.

Flies:— Traditional patterns.

Rogart Lochs

Permits:— Rogart Hotel, Rogart Angling Club

Between Lairg and Golspie in the Strath Brora area lies the picturesque area of Rogart. There are several lochs high in the hills of the estate near Scibercross, and the Club have stocked the loch with the unpronounceable name of *Loch Preas Nan Sgiathanach* with brook trout and day permits, possibly on Saturdays only, are available from Rogart Hotel. Bank fishing only. *Loch Muie* also available for bank fishing on weekdays.

Flies:— Traditional patterns.

—— ○ ——

SOME NOTES ON THE AUTHOR

Lesley Crawford is a committed Scot living and working from Reay on the Caithness and Sutherland border.

As a freelance journalist and photographer she regularly contributes to the magazine 'Salmon Trout and Sea-trout' and to other outdoor pursuit publications, such as 'Great Outdoors', 'Shooting and Conservation' and the 'Scottish Sporting Gazette' and newspapers such as the 'Press and Journal' and the 'Inverness Courier'.

As an active member of S.A.N.A. (Scottish Anglers National Association) she became the first S.A.N.A. qualified trout instructor north of Inverness in October 1989.

She has over 20 years experience of trout fishing throughout Scotland and is a keen conservationist and bird watcher and active in other outdoor pursuits such as hill walking and cycling.

———— O ————

SELECT BIBLIOGRAPHY

John Buckland et al:— 'Pocket Guide to Trout and Salmon Flies'.

Fraser Darling and J.M. Boyd:— 'Natural History in the Highlands and Islands'.

T.T. Macan & E.B. Worthington:— 'Life in Lakes and Rivers'.

John McEwan:— 'Who Owns Scotland'.

Moray McLaren and W.B. Currie:— 'The Fishing Waters of Scotland'.

Nature Conservancy Council:— 'Peatlands of Caithness and Sutherland'.

Nature Conservancy Council:— 'Nature Conservation and Afforestation in Britain'.

D. Omand et al:— 'Caithness — A Field Guide'.

Bruce Sandison:— 'Trout Lochs of Scotland'.

Colonel R. Venables:— 'The Experienced Angler'.

Tom Weir:— 'The Scottish Lochs'.

———— O ————

FINALE

And so there you have it. The lochs of Caithness and Sutherland and how best to tackle them. It only remains for me to wish you every success, and if perchance we meet I am the little one with the woolly hat and waders, sometimes casting determinedly, sometimes gazing into the firmament, but always, always loving every minute of it...

Lesley C Crawford

Askival

Reay

Caithness

ALPHABETICAL LIST OF LOCHS/AREAS

(S) = Sutherland   (C) = Caithness

A

Achaidh Mhoir
A'Choin
Ailsh
Airigh Bige
Airigh Leathaid
Airigh na Beinne
Airigh na Creige
Akran
Altnaharra
An Arbhair
An Lagain
Arichlinie
Assynt
Awe

B

Baddidarach
Badenloch
Bad an Fheur
Bad an Gallaig
Bad nan Aighean
Beannach
Bettyhill
Beul na Faire
Bhuldaidh
Borralan
Borralie
Breac Buidhe
Brora
Buidhe
Buidhe (Strathy)

C

Caise
Caladail
Calder
Cam

Caol (C)
Caol (S)
Caol (S)
Caorach
Cape Wrath
Chaoruinn
Cherigal
Coire nam Mang
Cormaic
Cracail
Craggie I (S)
Craggie II (S)
Craggie III (S)
Croispol
Cross
Culag
Cul Fraoich
Culiadh

D

Dherue
Dornoch
Doula
Druim a Chliabhain
Druim Suardalain
Drumbeg
Dubh
Dubn nan Geo
Dunnet Head Lochs
Durness

E

Eaglaise Beg
Eaglaise Mor
Earach
Eileanach (C)
Eileanach (S)
Eun

F

Fada
Farlary
Fearna
Fhionnaich
Fiag
Fionn
Forsinard

G

Gaineimh
Gainmich (S)
Garbh
Ghriama
Gillaroo
Glutt
Gorm Beg
Gorm Mor

H

Hakel
Heilan
Hempriggs
Hope
Horn

I

Inchnadamph
Inshore
Inver Lodge

K

Keisgaig
Kinlochbervie
Kyle of Sutherland

L

Laggan
Lanlish
Laoigh
Laro

Leir
Lily
Loyal
Lucy
Lundie

M

Meadie I (S)
Meadie II (S)
Meadie III (S)
Meala
Merkland
Mhuillin (C)
Mhuillin (C)
Mhuillin I (S)
Mhuillin II (S)
Migdale
Modsarie
Mor
Mor a chraisg
More (S)
More (C)
Muie

N

Nam Breac Buidhe
Nam Breac (Forsinard)
Nan Clar
Nan Clach
Nan Laogh
Naver

O

Olginey
Overscaig Hotel
Oykel Bridge Hotel

P

Plantation
Preas nan Sgiathanach

R

Rangag
Rhiconich
Rimsdale
Rogart
Ruard
Ruathair
Rumsdale

S

Sand
Sandwood
Saorach
Sarclet
Scarmclate
Scourie
Scrabster
Seilge (Shallag)
Shin
Shurrery
Skerrach
Skerray
Sletill
Slaim
Stack
Staink
Stemster
St Johns
Strathy

T

Talaheel
Tarvie
Thormaid
Thulachan
Tigh Choimhid
Tigh na Creige
Toftingall
Tolla Bhaid
Truderscaig

U

Uidh n Geadaig
Urigill

V

Veyatie

W

Watten
Wester

Y

Yarrows

RECORD OF FISH CAUGHT

NAME	DATE CAUGHT	APPROXIMATE WEIGHT	NOTES

RECORD OF FISH CAUGHT

NAME	DATE CAUGHT	APPROXIMATE WEIGHT	NOTES

NOTES